Martin Luther

A Reforming Spirit

Tamara Leigh Hollingsworth

Publishing Credits

Dona Herweck Rice, *Editor-in-Chief*
Lee Aucoin, *Creative Director*
Torrey Maloof, *Editor*
Neri Garcia, *Senior Designer*
Stephanie Reid, *Photo Researcher*
Rachelle Cracchiolo, M.S.Ed., *Publisher*

Image Credits

cover (left) Newscom, cover (right) Bridgeman Art Library; p.1 Newscom; p.4 Newscom; p.5 INTERFOTO/Alamy; p.6 The Granger Collection; p.7 Bridgeman Art Library; p.8 The Granger Collection; p.9 Bridgeman Art Library; p.10 Getty Images; p.11 The Granger Collection; p.12 Newscom; p.13 Bridgeman Art Library; p.14 Newscom; p.15 Newscom; p.16 Bridgeman Art Library; p.17 The Granger Collection;p.18 (top) INTERFOTO/Alamy, p.18 (bottom) Newscom; p.19 Mary Evans Picture Library/Alamy; p.20 Newscom; p.21 Bridgeman Art Library; p.22 (top) The Granger Collection, p.22 (bottom) Shutterstock, Inc.; p.23 Newscom; p.24 Mary Evans Picture Library/Alamy; p.25 Bridgeman Art Library; p.26 The Granger Collection; p.27 Newscom; p.28 Bridgeman Art Library; p.29 Shutterstock, Inc.; p.32 Newscom; back cover Newscom

---

Teacher Created Materials
5301 Oceanus Drive
Huntington Beach, CA 92649-1030
http://www.tcmpub.com

ISBN 978-1-4333-5010-8

Printed in China
Nordica.082019.CA21901024

Table of Contents

Father of the Reformation

On October 31, 1517, an ordinary man dressed in a brown monk's robe walked through a town in Wittenberg, Germany. The people around did not pay much attention to the man. He walked to the front door of Castle Church and posted a piece of paper on the door. Then, he turned and walked away. This one action would change the course of history.

The man's name was Martin Luther (LOO-ther). The paper he nailed to the church door created a lot of **controversy**. It raised many questions that would change the way people lived and what they believed. It would inspire some people and upset others. It would challenge the rulers and give power to the **commoners**. But most importantly, his words would start the **Reformation** (ref-er-MEY-shuhn).

the Catholic hierarchy: the pope, cardinals, bishops, and priests

The Reformation caused many changes in Europe in the 1500s. For a thousand years, the Roman Catholic Church ruled all of Europe. It had rules and laws and a **hierarchy** (HAHY-uh-rahr-kee) like a modern-day government. The Reformation would question this power and many of the beliefs of the Catholic Church.

Catholic Structure

The Catholic Church had an organized hierarchy. The leader was the pope. Under the pope were cardinals, bishops, and priests. Common people who were not part of the clergy formed the lowest group in the hierarchy.

Gutenberg Printing Press

In 1440, Johann Gutenberg (YOH-hahn GOOT-n-burg) created a printing press that could make books faster and cheaper than ever before. The printing press also allowed more books to be published in the **vernacular**, or language of the commoners, instead of Latin. This helped more people learn to read. As more people were able to read, the more they were able to talk about important issues of the day.

Young Luther

Living in a Catholic World

On November 10, 1483, in Eisleben (AIS-lee-buhn), Germany, the Luther family welcomed a baby boy to the world. Just like all Catholic families, they took their newborn son to the local church to be **baptized**. It was a tradition at that time to name the child in honor of the saint who was celebrated on the day a child was baptized. This is how Martin Luther got his name. He was baptized on the day that honored Saint Martin de Tours.

It was important to Luther's parents that their son be part of the Church. The world in which Luther was born was harsh. Crime and sickness were common. Most people were poor and hungry. Since the Catholic Church was powerful and wealthy, it could help people when they were in trouble. However, with this power came fear.

An infant is baptized.

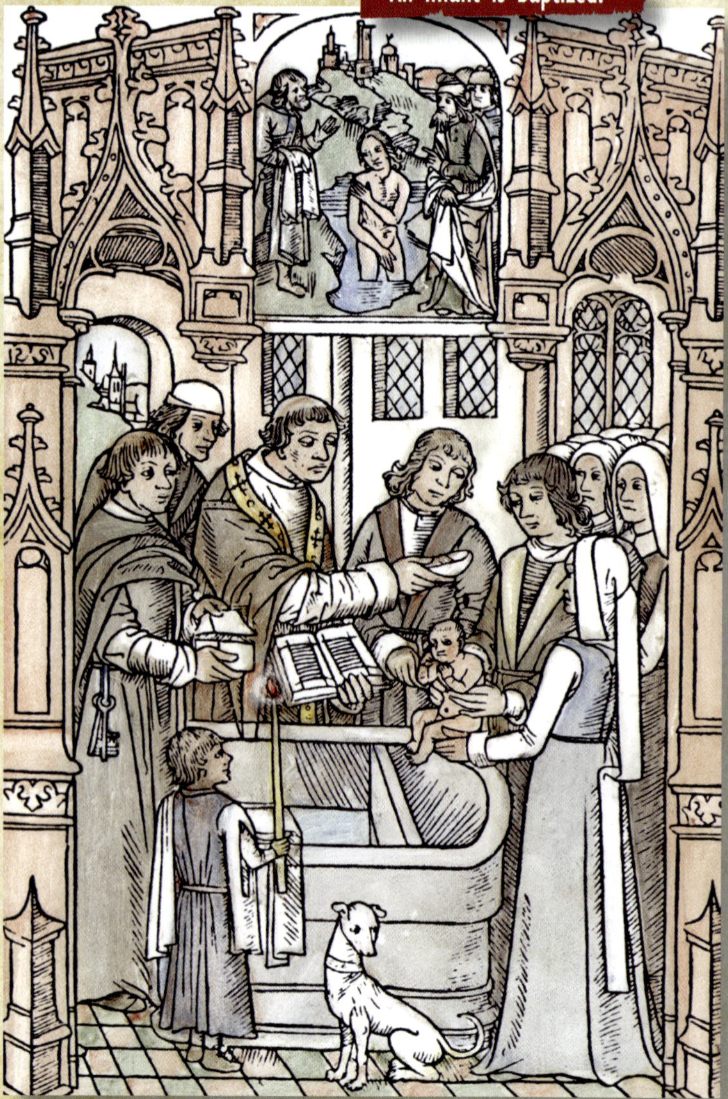

People were fearful of angering the Church. The Church often portrayed God as angry. It thought that people deserved the bad things that happened to them because of their **sins**. Sins are thoughts and actions that go against the laws of God. People believed that the Catholic leaders spoke for God. Therefore, they were afraid the leaders would say that God was angry with them.

the Black Death

Baptism

The Catholic Church believes that babies need to be baptized soon after they are born. During a baptism, a baby is taken to the local church where a priest pours a small amount of holy water onto the baby's head. This water is meant to wash the baby clean from sin.

Black Death

A horrible illness called the Black Death had moved through Europe just before Luther was born. It had killed hundreds of thousands of people. It was named the Black Death because people's skin often had a blackish color when they got the sickness. Many people thought that the illness was sent from God as a punishment for their sins.

Erfurt, Germany

A Promise Kept

Luther spent his childhood trying to be a good boy. His father wanted Luther to become a lawyer to help support the family. Luther did not want to go to law school, but he did to honor his father's wishes. He went to the University of Erfurt (AIR-fohrt) in Germany.

On a humid day in July 1505, Luther was on his way to class when a violent thunderstorm struck. In fear he cried out, "Saint Anne, help me! I will become a monk!" When he arrived safely, Luther decided to keep his promise.

Two weeks later, Luther entered the Black Cloister (KLOI-ster). This was an Augustinian (aw-guh-STIN-ee-uhn) **monastery**. Augustinian monks followed the lifestyle of a saint named Augustine. Saint Augustine preached that people were born sinful and could not become fit for heaven without God's help.

Luther was a good monk. He followed the rules of the monastery. He tried to live perfectly in order to earn God's favor. But no matter how hard he tried, Luther still did not feel worthy of heaven.

Luther studies in a monastery in Erfurt.

Monks and Nuns

A monk is male, while a nun is female. There are different types of monks and nuns in the Catholic Church. However, they all follow the basic belief of poverty and celibacy (SEL-uh-buh-see). Poverty means that they work for others instead of themselves. Celibacy means that they will never marry and have children.

Religion, Medicine, or Law?

When Luther lived, only men were allowed to attend school. When a male student started college, he could choose to study medicine, law, or religion. No other types of classes were offered.

Struggling with Faith

Travels to Rome

At the Black Cloister, Luther had a loving friend and **mentor** named Johann von Staupitz (YOH-hahn vahn SHTOW-pits). Staupitz sent Luther to teach a class at a new school in Wittenberg. Luther prayed and studied. He did physical **penance**, such as not allowing himself food or comfort. Still, Luther did not feel holy enough for God.

In 1510, Staupitz had Luther join a group of monks traveling to Rome, Italy, the holiest city for Catholics. In Rome, Luther would be able to meet holy men, experience the holy city, and touch holy items. Luther hoped visiting Rome would help him get closer to heaven.

While in Rome, Luther became even more confused. He felt honored to see the holy **relics**, or items, but was horrified to see how the religious men of Rome lived. Luther had grown up poor, like most common people at the time. But here, the priests, bishops, and cardinals lived like kings. These men were supposed to be closer to God than anyone else on Earth. Yet, Luther saw that these men did not lead simple lives. He began to have more doubts about the Catholic Church and his own faith.

Johann von Staupitz

Luther at work in Rome

Rome, Italy

Rome was the most important city for Catholics. The pope, the leader of the Catholic faith, lived in Rome. There were many relics in Rome, and people would travel hundreds of miles to see them. People believed that seeing these items would help them earn God's favor.

Penance

Penance was very important in the Catholic Church. When someone sinned, he or she would confess, or tell his or her sins, to a priest. The priest would tell the person to do penance to prove they were sorry. Catholics believed penance would help them earn God's forgiveness for their sins.

A New Philosophy

When Luther returned from Rome, he had a **crisis** in his heart and mind. He wondered if he could ever do enough penance to earn God's love.

Von Staupitz wanted to keep Luther busy. He told Luther to earn another degree. Luther did. He graduated in 1512. He taught classes and was in charge of 11 monasteries. He began to lock himself away to study the Bible. For five years, he searched the words of the Bible for answers to the questions that haunted him.

Martin Luther teaching

A man receives salvation before he is crucified.

Luther's studies changed his beliefs. He no longer thought that people needed to do penance to earn **salvation**, or entrance to heaven. Luther said that forgiving sins and giving **grace** was God's work. God gives grace to people for free, without expecting something in return. This idea was called ***justification***. Justification means people are **purged**, or washed, of their sins if they believe in Jesus Christ. Luther said that people are justified by grace alone, not by their deeds. All people had to do to get to heaven, he said, was have faith in Jesus Christ.

Catholic Afterlife

Catholics believe there are three places people can go when they die. One is heaven, a place of joy and closeness to God. Another is hell, a place of punishment for sins. The area between is called ***purgatory*** (PUR-guh-tawr-ee). Purgatory is a place where a person's sins are purged from them so that they can go to heaven eventually.

God's Grace

The Catholic Church believed that a person needed to do good deeds to be saved. Luther's new idea about grace was that it was God's free gift to people who had faith. People did not have to earn salvation. God gave it to them for free.

Sparking Change

Luther's Ninety-Five Theses

In 1517, the pope was building a huge **cathedral** in Rome. To raise money, he sent church leaders to sell **indulgences**. An indulgence was a piece of paper people could buy. On the paper, the pope stated that the person would not have to spend as much time in purgatory. People bought indulgences for themselves or a loved one to help them get to heaven faster.

Luther posts his Ninety-Five Theses on the door at Castle Church.

Luther thought it was wrong to sell indulgences. He believed that only God could decide what happened to people when they die. At first, Luther did little more than preach against selling indulgences. But later, Luther became angry when some of the members of his church started buying indulgences.

Luther decided to write a list of Ninety-Five Theses (THEE-seez). These were topics that he wanted people to discuss. He posted this list on the door of Castle Church in the center of Wittenberg, Germany. Some of the issues on Luther's list included grace, justification, and indulgences. Posting ideas for debate was common at this time. Luther just wanted to begin a discussion. Instead, he started the Reformation.

selling indulgences

Tetzel's Commercials

Nobody was more skilled at selling indulgences than Johann Tetzel (TET-suhl). He was an excellent salesman. Parades and music would announce his arrival in a town. He even had his own popular saying, "As soon as the coin in the **coffer** rings, a soul from purgatory springs!" Luther thought that selling indulgences was an abuse of power. He argued that once God gave a person grace, there was no need for purgatory or indulgences.

Luther's Words Spread

The Catholic Church started when the Romans were in power. The Church still held onto the customs from that time. One of those customs was the Latin language. All Church writing was in Latin. This practice **isolated**, or set apart, the Church from the common people.

When Luther posted his Ninety-Five Theses, people **translated** his ideas into other languages. One of those languages was German. Now, the common people could read and think about Luther's theses. It was the first time the common people could question their leaders. It was not long before many people began to question the way the Church was run.

Luther preaches about the importance of translation.

Germans discuss Luther's Ninety-Five Theses.

Luther thought his ideas would only create a debate among Church leaders. When the pope heard the news that many people were being influenced by Luther's writings, he thought little of it. However, when the pope saw that the money he needed from indulgences was not coming in, he quickly changed his mind. The pope asked one of his men to meet with Luther. The pope wanted Luther to **recant**, or take back, what he said in his theses.

The Vernacular

The writings of the Catholic Church were in Latin. But, the people of the Holy Roman Empire spoke different languages. People in France spoke French, and people in Germany spoke German. When the Ninety-Five Theses were translated into the vernacular (ver-NAK-yuh-ler), the language of the common people, it made Luther's ideas available to more people.

Accidental Revolutionary

When Luther posted his Ninety-Five Theses on the church door, he was not trying to start a religious revolution. If he wanted common people to read his theses, he would have written them in German. Instead, he wrote them in Latin so that only the educated church leaders could read them.

Holding Firm in Faith

Recant or Excommunication

In August 1518, Luther received a message ordering him to come to Augsburg, Germany. He was to meet with Cardinal Cajetan (KAH-juh-tun). Cajetan was the second-most powerful person in the entire Catholic world. He would decide if Luther was guilty of **heresy** (HER-uh-see). Heresy, or ideas that went against Church doctrine, was harshly punished.

A terrified Luther met with the cardinal. Luther knelt and showed respect to Cajetan. When Cajetan asked Luther to recant his beliefs, Luther refused. That night, fearing for his life, Luther fled to Wittenberg. For a few months after the meeting with Cajetan, nothing happened. The pope issued a notice declaring the Church had a right to sell indulgences.

Luther meets with Cardinal Cajetan.

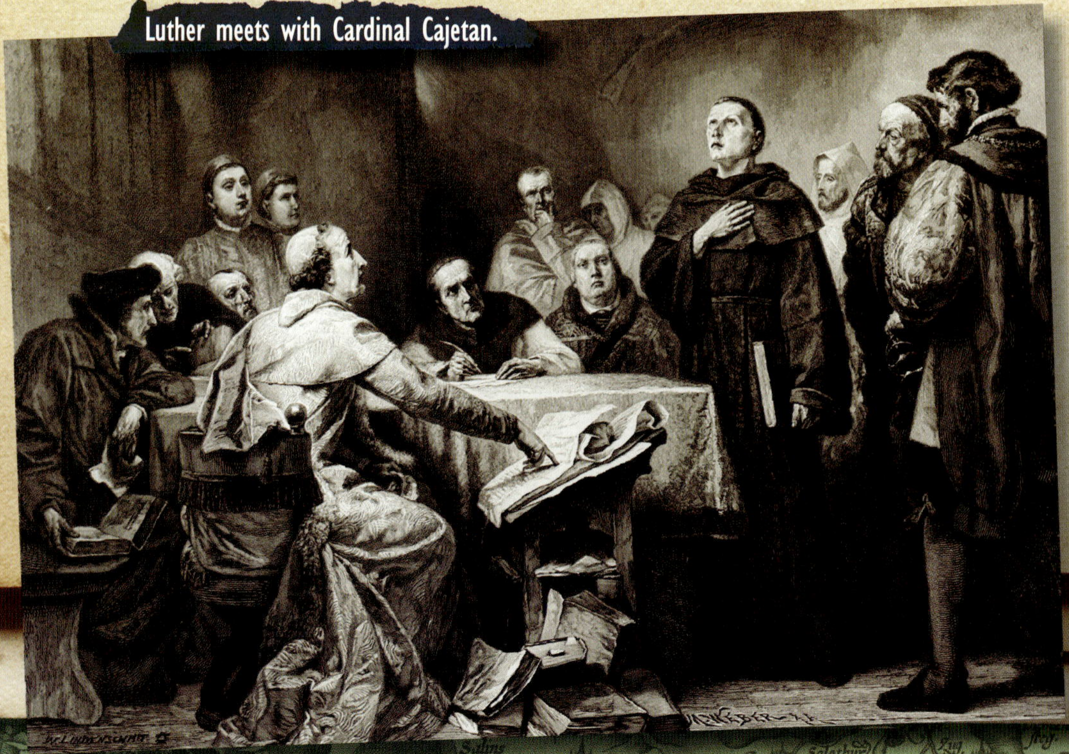

Luther meets Johann Eck.

The pope also set up a debate between Luther and a man named Johann Eck for the people to watch. Armed guards were called in to protect the men during their lengthy debate. The crowds of people who had watched the debate were interested in Luther's ideas. His classes became filled with students. His books started selling out. In response, the pope issued a statement demanding that Luther recant his words. If Luther did not recant, he would be **excommunicated** (eks-kuh-MYOO-ni-keyt-id).

Excommunication

To be excommunicated from the Church meant that a person could no longer be involved in anything the Church did. They could not baptize their children. They could not get married. And, most importantly, they could not go to heaven.

Luther and Eck

Martin Luther and Johann Eck were very good friends at one time. However, Luther and Eck did not agree about grace. Eck wrote Luther letters trying to show him where he believed Luther had been wrong. After their debate, Eck called Luther a heretic, or someone who has ideas that go against a religion.

Johann Eck

Diet of Worms

In 1521, a special meeting called a *diet* was held in the city of Worms (vawrms), Germany. The Catholic Church and monarchy worked together to establish laws. They met at these meetings every few years to discuss and resolve issues. One of the main concerns at this meeting was Luther. His ideas had spread all over Europe. Some worried that if the pope excommunicated him without speaking to Luther himself, it might cause a **revolt**. So, Luther was invited to attend a meeting called the *Diet of Worms*.

Luther at the Diet of Worms

When Luther entered the room, he looked around. He was surrounded by the most powerful men in the Western world. In the center of the room was a table stacked with his books. Luther was asked if he had written the books. He stated that the books were his. Luther was also asked if he still believed all the ideas presented in his books. Luther said he needed to pray before he could answer.

Der Römischen Kaiserlichē Maiestat Edict wider Martin Luthers

the Edict of Worms

The next day, Luther refused to recant his ideas. Church leaders issued a formal notice called the *Edict of Worms*. The edict, or order, excommunicated Luther. It made him a criminal.

Edict of Worms

The Edict of Worms officially excommunicated Luther from the Catholic Church. It outlined rules stating that any person could arrest Luther. It made it a law for people to turn Luther in if they saw him.

"My Conscience is Captive"

When church leaders asked Luther if he would recant his writings, Luther said the following: "My conscience is captive to the Word of God. Thus I cannot and will not recant, because acting against one's conscience is neither safe nor sound. God help me. Amen." Luther meant that people should not be ashamed of their beliefs.

Wartburg Castle

Living in Secret

Luther left Worms that afternoon. For many days, people listened to him preach. But one day, he was gone. The three men who had been traveling with him said that Luther had been kidnapped. Some people thought that Luther was dead. However, Luther was living. He was hidden away in the castle of his friend Frederick.

To keep safe, Luther hid himself from the public view. He took off his priest's clothes and dressed as a knight. He changed his name to Junker Jörg (YUHNK-er yorg). He remained in the castle for 10 months. He spent almost all of his time indoors praying and writing. During this time he translated the New Testament of the Bible into German. This translation would become a best seller. It was the first time that many Germans were able to read the Bible.

Luther knew he needed to come out of hiding when he saw the confusion and **rebellion** that had come from the Edict of Worms. Even though he had never intended to, Luther's ideas had started a **revolution**.

Junker Jörg

The name Luther adopted when he went into hiding was Junker Jörg. This means Knight George. Unlike his days as a monk, Luther grew out his hair and beard. He wore fine clothes and lived in comfort.

Wartburg Castle

Wartburg (VAHRT-boork) Castle was where Luther hid while he was Junker Jörg. While he lived there, Luther spent most of his time writing about his beliefs. He described that experience as feeling like he "fought the Devil with ink." Wartburg Castle still stands today.

Luther translates the Bible.

Luther's chamber in Wartburg Castle

Luther tries to stop the Peasants' War.

Different Goals

All across Europe, common people began to rebel against the Church. People burned churches. They fought against their leaders. They demanded church reform. Every group had a different goal. The wealthy wanted the Church to have less power. The peasants wanted to have more freedom from the wealthy. Many people wanted the Church to change its beliefs.

the Peasants' War

Luther was sad when he saw the **conflict**. He returned to Wittenberg and tried to calm the people. He preached patience. He urged people not to be violent. Luther taught **equality**. He believed that all people were equal in God's eyes. Luther tried to get people to focus on changing the Church's beliefs, but many people wanted social and political change more.

In 1525, peasants used Luther's idea of equality to demand more rights. When they did not get them, they used violence to make their point. Luther criticized the peasants. He even went so far as to tell those in power to punish them. This bloody battle was called the *Peasants' War*.

Other Voices

When Luther went into hiding, other people began to speak out against the Church. These leaders helped spread the Reformation to other countries around Europe.

Catholic Reformation

The Catholic Church saw that Luther's words meant something to the people. Trying to bring people back to the Church, they began something called the Catholic Reformation, or Counter-Reformation. This movement worked to change some of the problems people pointed out during the Reformation.

A Different Life

Marriage and Family

Luther felt he could not control the dramatic changes that were taking place. He continued to preach and work with the members of his church. However, he tried to stay away from public view. In 1525, he married a woman named Katharina von Bora (BOOR-uh). Luther called her Katie.

Katie had been a nun until she read some of Luther's books. She believed in his writings and decided to leave the Church. Like most of what Luther did, his marriage was a point of great debate. The Catholic Church did not allow priests to marry. Some saw Luther's marriage as an act of **defiance**. Others believed that Luther had every right to be married.

Luther marries Katharina.

Protestant

A variety of new religious groups were created because of the Reformation. These new church groups, or denominations, all have their own name, but as a whole they are called Protestant. It comes from the word *protest,* since the movement started by protesting the Catholic Church's beliefs and practices.

Marriage

Luther's marriage changed the rules. In the Catholic Church, priests and nuns are not allowed to marry. However, today in Protestant denominations, ministers and preachers are allowed to marry and have families. This is because Luther did it first.

the Luther family

The Luthers always seemed to have a full house. They gave birth to six children and adopted four more. Their home rang with the talk of children, as well as that of many students and visitors.

Luther's ideas spread quickly around Europe. Even though he was becoming an old man, he never seemed to stop working. He continued preaching, writing, and traveling. Luther kept sharing his ideas with others until his death in 1546. He was 62 years old.

Luther's Legacy

On the day of his funeral, the city of Wittenberg was full of people. The streets were lined with Luther's followers. Castle Church was packed. Some people loved Luther and the freedom they thought he brought to them. Others hated him for criticizing the Church. Today, Luther is still controversial because of the things that he taught.

Luther spent much of his life trying to understand how to be good enough to earn God's favor. When he felt he had found the answer, he shared his findings with those who would listen. Luther proclaimed his beliefs loudly for all to hear. When Church leaders told him to recant, Luther held firm to his beliefs.

Luther never wanted to start a movement that would take on the most powerful institution in the world. But he did. He started a Reformation that would spread around Europe and the world. His writings challenged the Church's beliefs and practices.

Today, almost every church bears some kind of mark of the Reformation that Luther started. Luther's thoughts fueled a fire that changed world history.

Luther on his deathbed

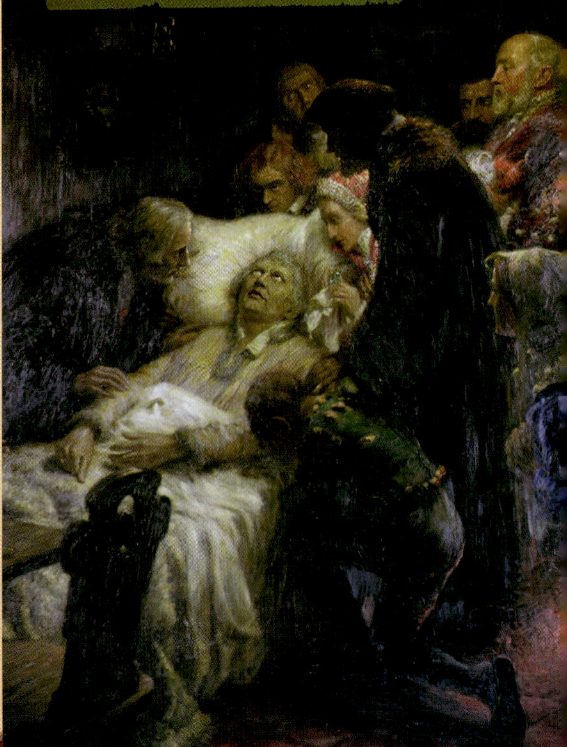

a statue of Martin Luther in Germany

Catholic Reforms

The Catholic Church did not resist change entirely during this period. Catholic leaders ended some of the abuses of power, such as the selling of indulgences. But the Catholic Church refused to change its views of faith and good deeds.

Heirs of the Reformation

Today, there are many different denominations and churches that came about because of the Reformation. Lutheran churches follow the tradition of Martin Luther. Presbyterian (prez-bi-TEER-ee-uhn) and Reformed churches follow the tradition of John Calvin. Baptist churches loosely follow the legacy of the Anabaptists. And Episcopalians (ih-pis-kuh-PEYL-yuhnz) follow the tradition of the Church of England.

Glossary

baptized—made pure through a ceremony in which a person is sprinkled with water

cathedral—a large and important church

coffer—a small box for keeping money or valuables

commoners—people with little money or power

conflict—an extended struggle

controversy—a fight or debate of ideas

crisis—a difficult time when things are unsure, often leading to a choice

defiance—to openly and willingly disobey the rules

equality—to be the same in terms of rights

excommunicated—cut off from the Catholic Church

grace—a gift that is not earned, but given, usually by God

heresy—a religious belief that goes against the church

hierarchy—an organization in which people or things are ranked above or below each other

indulgences—papers that could be purchased and were believed to shorten a soul's time in purgatory

isolated—set apart

justification—being made right with God; being cleansed from sins

mentor—a person who inspires you and works to help you succeed

monastery—a place where monks live

penance—an act someone does to show they are sorry for their sins

purgatory—in Roman Catholicism, a place where souls are made pure from sin after death

purged—made something pure

rebellion—an act or thought against the person or ideas in charge

recant—to take back something already spoken aloud

Reformation—a movement in the 1500s that called for changes in the Roman Catholic Church

relics—items that have historical or religious importance

revolt—to rise up against a power

revolution— a dramatic change in society

salvation—the saving of a person from sin or hell

sins—doing something to break God's law; bad or wicked acts

translated—changed from one language to another

vernacular—the language spoken by the common people

Index

Your Turn!

In 1517, Martin Luther began questioning many practices of the Catholic Church and its leader, the pope. Luther wrote a list of Ninety-Five Theses that he wanted people to discuss. He posted the list on the door of Castle Church in the center of Wittenberg, Germany. Some of the issues on Luther's list included grace, justification, and indulgences. Luther wanted to make people think.

Spreading the News

Imagine that you are a printer in the town of Wittenburg, Germany, in November of 1517. A priest and scholar named Martin Luther caused quite a stir with his Ninety-Five Theses. Write a headline and short article about the event to spread the news.